RIVER LIFE

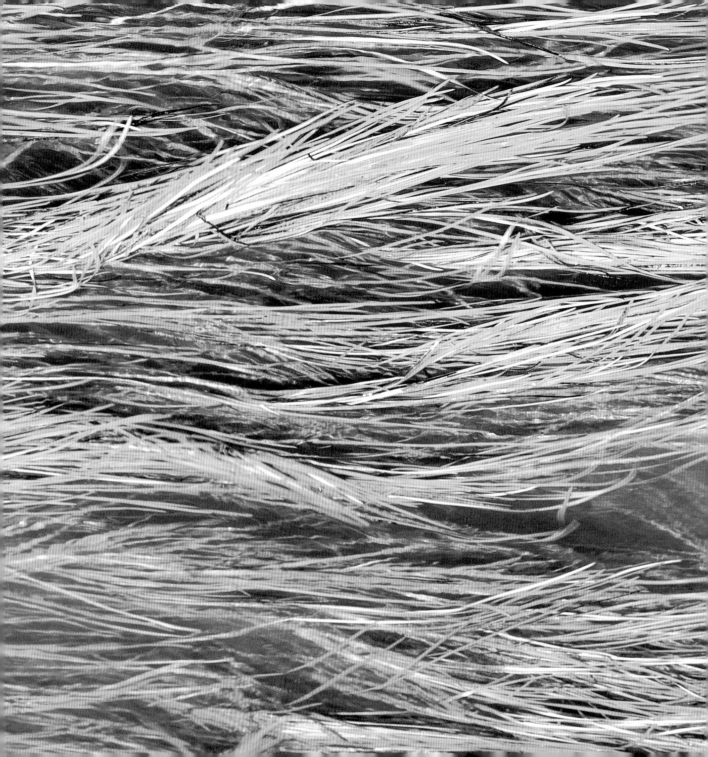

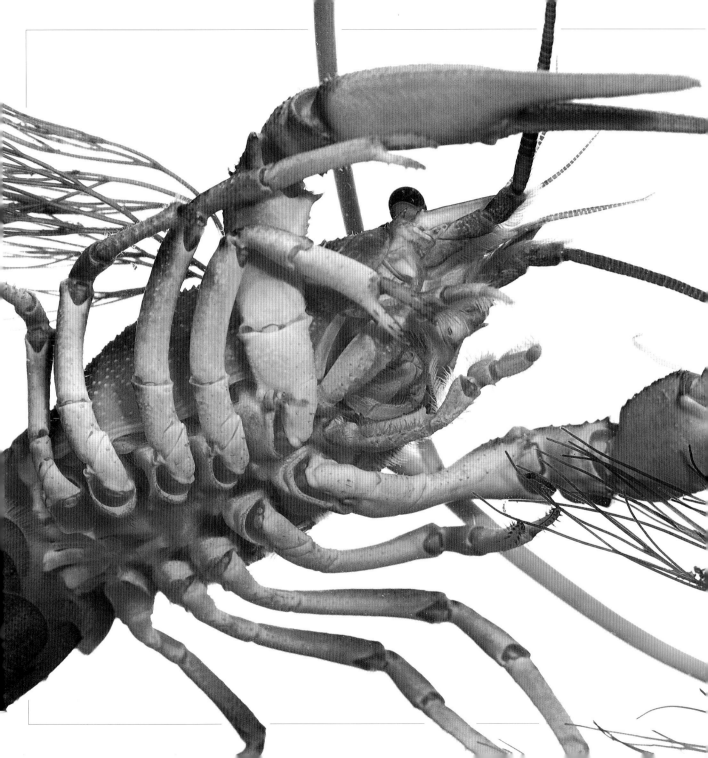

RIVER LIFE

PHOTOGRAPHED BY
FRANK GREENAWAY

WRITTEN BY
BARBARA TAYLOR

DK PUBLISHING, INC.

A DK PUBLISHING BOOK

Senior editor Christiane Gunzi **Senior art editor** Val Wright
Editor Sue Copsey **Art editor** Julie Staniland
Design assistant Lucy Bennett
Production Louise Barratt
Illustrations Nick Hall
Index Jane Parker
Managing editor Sophie Mitchell
Managing art editor Miranda Kennedy
U.S. editor B. Alison Weir

Consultants
Paul Clarke, Andy Currant, Theresa Greenaway,
Paul Hillyard, Gordon Howes, Tim Parmenter, Edward Wade

With thanks to Jane Burton, Ben Dawson, Trevor Smith's Animal World, and Neil
Welton (Dorking Aquatic Centre) for supplying some of the animals in this book.

First American Edition, 1992
First Paperback Edition, 1998
2 4 6 8 10 9 7 5 3

Published in the United States by
DK Publishing, Inc., 95 Madison Avenue, New York, New York, 10016.
Visit us on the World Wide Web at http://www.dk.com

Library of Congress Cataloging-in-Publication Data
Taylor, Barbara, 1954-
River life/photographed by Frank Greenaway, written by Barbara Taylor.
p. cm. – (Look closer)
Includes index.
Summary: Examines, in text and photographs, the animals and plants that live in and along a river.
ISBN 0-7894-3478-4
1. Stream fauna–Juvenile literature. [1. Stream animals. 2. Stream plants. 3. Rivers.]
I. Greenaway, Frank, ill. II. Title. III. Series
QL145.T39 1992
591.92'9–dc20
92-52822–CIP–AC

Colour reproduction by Colourscan, Singapore
Printed and bound in China by L.Rex Printing Co., Ltd.

CONTENTS

Look for us, and we will show you the size of every animal and plant that you read about in this book.

LIFE IN A RIVER

FROM COLD, RUSHING TORRENTS to warm, sluggish tropical waters, the rivers of the world contain a wealth of wildlife. Plants take root in the soft, damp soil of the riverbank, and animals dig burrows to live in. Many insect larvae live under the water, while the adults find a mate and feed above the surface. These flying insects are eagerly snapped up by hungry birds and bats. Many rivers have been polluted by poisonous chemicals and wastes from factories, farms, and houses. We need to clean up our rivers and stop using them as dumping grounds, so that wildlife and people can go on enjoying the rivers for years to come.

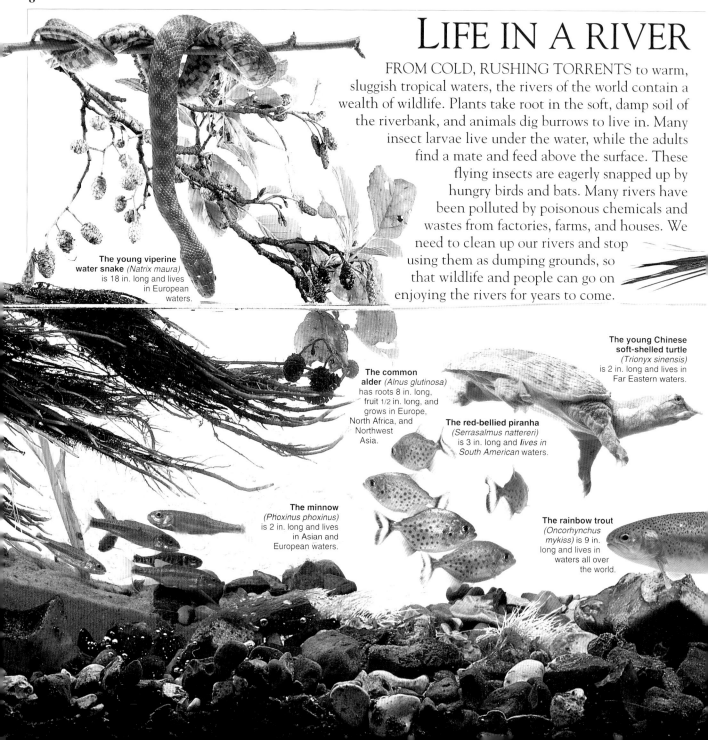

The young viperine water snake *(Natrix maura)* is 18 in. long and lives in European waters.

The young Chinese soft-shelled turtle *(Trionyx sinensis)* is 2 in. long and lives in Far Eastern waters.

The common alder *(Alnus glutinosa)* has roots 8 in. long, fruit 1/2 in. long, and grows in Europe, North Africa, and Northwest Asia.

The red-bellied piranha *(Serrasalmus nattereri)* is 3 in. long and *lives in South American* waters.

The minnow *(Phoxinus phoxinus)* is 2 in. long and lives in Asian and European waters.

The rainbow trout *(Oncorhynchus mykiss)* is 9 in. long and lives in waters all over the world.

The Daubenton's bat *(Myotis daubentonii)* has a wingspan of 10 in., and lives in Asia and Europe.

The mayfly's *(Ephemera danica)* body is 1 in. long, and it lives in Europe and other Mediterrean countries.

The gray wagtail *(Motacilla cinerea)* is 7 in. long and lives in Africa, Europe, India, Iran, and Southeast Asia.

The young brown rat's *(Rattus norvegicus)* body is 4 in. long, and it lives all over the world.

The European crayfish *(Austropotamobius pallipes)* is 4 in. long and lives in Western European waters.

The young big-headed turtle *(Platysternon megacephalum)* is 3 1/2 in. long and lives in Southeast Asian waters.

WALKING UNDER WATER

CRAYFISH LIVE IN LAKES and rivers, but can only survive if the water is clean. They are related to the lobsters that live in the sea. Like crabs and other crustaceans, a crayfish has a protective outer coat, called an exoskeleton, which it makes from chalk in the water. During the day, crayfish hide under stones, among weeds, or in a burrow in the riverbank. At night, they walk along the river bottom, feeding on snails, worms, and insect larvae (grubs). Crayfish mate in the autumn, and the female lays about 100 pink eggs. She carries them under her body for up to six months. In spring, the eggs hatch and the young crayfish cling to the female's tiny swimming legs, called swimmerets. One or two weeks later, they are ready to leave their mother.

GUESS WHAT?
A crayfish can grow new legs and pincers if one breaks off. That's why one pincer is sometimes longer than the other.

REVERSE GEAR
When the crayfish flicks its tail forward, it moves backward through the water at high speed. This helps it escape from danger and swim against strong currents in the river. Underneath its abdomen are special legs for swimming, called swimmerets, which it uses to move itself forward.

Close up, you can see tiny hairs on the body. These sense movements in the water, and help the crayfish avoid danger.

The broad tail is shaped like a fan to push the water aside.

The hard exoskeleton is divided into segments so that the crayfish can bend.

There are eight legs attached to the thorax.

Claws on the legs and pincers grasp things and pull the crayfish along the riverbed.

PINCER POWER

The first pair of legs are larger and heavier than the others, forming pincers called chelipeds. The male crayfish mainly uses its chelipeds for defense, and to hold on to the female during mating. It also uses them to dig burrows.

MOLTING AND MUNCHING

The crayfish's hard outer skin, called the exoskeleton, will not stretch. So the animal must molt (shed its skin) every so often in order to grow. The old exoskeleton usually comes off in one piece, and the crayfish eats it for the vitamins and minerals that it contains. While the crayfish waits for its soft new skin to harden, it hides out of the way of predators.

The two smaller antennae are divided into two branches. They can sense chemicals in the water as well as movement.

The top part of the exoskeleton is called the carapace.

The two large compound eyes can see well, even in dark water.

This jagged point is called the rostrum. It juts out from the carapace to protect the front of the head.

Each antenna is made up of lots of segments so that it can bend.

These long antennae detect movements in the water and help the crayfish find food.

These joints allow the legs to bend for walking.

Males have larger chelipeds (pincers) than females. They use them mainly for defense.

LIFE IN THE FAST LANE

TROUT AND MINNOWS PREFER to live in clear, fast-flowing rivers and streams. Trout swim upriver to lay their eggs, which hatch in the spring. The females lay their eggs in the gravel of the riverbed. After about five weeks, young fish called fry hatch out and feed on water insects that drift past them. They take two or three years to develop into adults. Minnows usually shelter in quieter pools close to the riverbanks. They feed mainly on water insects. Although minnows are small fish, the female can lay up to 1,000 eggs. She lays them between stones to prevent them from being swept away by the current.

GUESS WHAT?
Minnows and trout can only live in clean water, so if you see them in a river or lake, you know that it is unpolluted.

BREEDING TIME
During the summer, in the breeding season, minnows often swim together in large groups, called schools. The males change into their breeding colors to attract a female. Their heads turn green, their bellies scarlet, and their sides greenish gold.

Dark markings help disguise the minnow.

The body is streamlined to help the fish swim fast.

The lateral line runs along the sides of the body.

The tail fin pushes the fish along and helps it steer.

Minnows push their jaws forward to gobble up small insects and other water creatures. Sometimes they also eat plants.

GIANT JAWS
Trout have large jaws with a
row of sharp teeth. When the
teeth wear out, new ones grow
to replace them. Like all fish,
trout gulp down their food
without chewing it first.

The large
eyes spot
food and
danger.

Black spots on the
trout's back
help it disappear
into the stones
and gravel on
the riverbed.

FISHING LINE
All fish have a special organ, called
a lateral line, which senses
vibrations (movements) in the
water. This helps the fish find its
way, avoid danger, and detect food.

Close up, you
can see the
protective
scales which
cover the body.

The teeth point
backward to
stop food from
wriggling away
before the fish
can swallow it.

A bony cover
protects the gills
underneath.

A BREATH OF FRESH WATER
Trout and minnows breathe by
taking in mouthfuls of water, which
they force over the gills in the
throat. The gills take in oxygen from
the water flowing over them. The
water is then forced out through a
flap which covers the gills.

These fanlike
pectoral fins help
the trout swim up
toward the surface,
and down into
deeper water.

TAIL TWITCHER

THE BUSY LITTLE gray wagtail walks along the edge of rushing mountain streams, or perches on rocks that stick up out of the water. When the wagtail spots an insect to eat, it quickly darts out to grab a meal. If it senses danger, it flies into the air, making a loud alarm call to warn other wagtails. In spring and summer, the male wagtail develops a black throat, which helps him attract a female. He makes a special display flight from tree to tree, flicking his wings, fluffing up his feathers, and fanning out his tail. The female lays between four and six eggs in a nest of moss and grass, lined with animal hair. The nest is always close to the water. After two weeks the young hatch out of the eggs. They are helpless at first, but develop quickly and can fly when they are just 17 days old.

Close up, you can see the lines of barbs on each feather, which are hooked tightly together.

The feathers at the tips of the wings are spread out to help the bird balance as it flies.

The outer feathers on the wing are for steering, like the flaps on an airplane's wing.

The wagtail uses its tail for balance, and for steering when it flies.

FEATHERY FACTS

A bird's feathers fit closely together over its body, making it a smooth, streamlined shape. The flight feathers are strong but bendable, so they do not snap when the bird twists its wings. The number of feathers on a bird changes according to the time of year. In the cold of winter, there are many more feathers than during the summer.

The large, beady eyes keep a lookout for insects and danger.

Sharp claws grip on to slippery surfaces, such as wet rocks and branches.

The wagtail keeps its nest clean by dropping old and dirty material into the river.

Inside the chest there are powerful muscles that beat the wings up and down.

WINGS AT WORK
A wagtail's wings are light and strong, and they bend easily. Unlike the wings on an airplane, which are fixed, a bird's wings can bend to help it twist and turn through the air. The wings are also slightly curved on top. This shape helps pull the bird upward as it flaps its wings up and down.

GUESS WHAT?
This bird is called a wagtail because its long tail wags up and down whenever and wherever it is perched.

IN-FLIGHT MEALS
The wagtail eats insects such as flies, midges, small dragonflies, and water beetles. It snaps them up with its long, pointed beak, which is a special shape for catching and holding on to wriggling insects. The wagtail often catches insects when it is in flight, especially over water.

The long beak snaps up insects as the wagtail flies along.

The feathers sometimes get wet as the bird skims low over the water.

TOE CLAMP
Wagtails have one toe pointing backward, and three toes pointing forward. This helps them grip on to branches. When a wagtail lands on a branch, its weight makes its toes clamp tightly shut so that it does not fall off its perch.

SHELLY SWIMSUIT

RIVER TURTLES LIVE in a variety of freshwater habitats, from still, shallow waters to rushing rivers. They are very similar to their relatives, the tortoises, which live on land. Like tortoises, they have a solid outer shell, as well as a bony skeleton inside their bodies. The shell of a river turtle is usually flatter and lighter than the shell of a tortoise. It is also a more streamlined shape, which helps the turtle glide quickly and smoothly through the water. Turtles court and mate in the water, but lay their eggs on land. They usually dig a hole with their back feet, bury the eggs, and then leave them. Turtles do not look after their eggs or young. A hatching turtle uses the hard point on its snout, called an egg tooth, to break its way out of the egg. It takes several years for it to become an adult.

GUESS WHAT?
Turtles have lived on Earth for more than 250 million years, since the days of the dinosaurs. Today's turtles look very similar to their ancestors, although the first turtles had teeth.

ARMOR PLATING
A turtle's shell is made up of bony plates that grow in the outer layer of its skin. On top of the plates are large, horny scales, called scutes. The top part of the shell, called the carapace, covers the turtle's back. The lower part, called the plastron, covers its belly. The carapace and plastron are joined together to make a box of armor around the turtle's soft body.

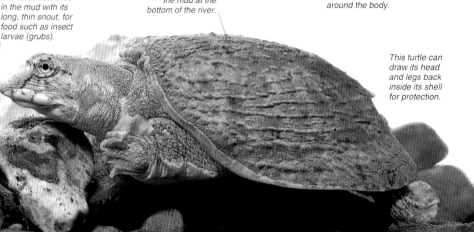

This long, flexible tail balances and steers the turtle.

SNORKEL SNOUT
Turtles need to come to the surface to breathe in air. This young Chinese soft-shelled turtle uses its long snout like a snorkel, poking it out of the water as it swims along or rests beneath the surface.

Large, webbed feet push the turtle through the water.

Sharp claws grip on to wet, slippery surfaces.

The legs are flattened, like paddles, for swimming.

The flattened shape of its shell allows this turtle to hide in the mud at the bottom of the river.

The plastron and carapace join to form a protective box around the body.

The turtle searches in the mud with its long, thin snout, for food such as insect larvae (grubs).

Sturdy legs support the weight of the shell.

This turtle can draw its head and legs back inside its shell for protection.

SOFT AND SPEEDY
A soft-shelled turtle has no horny outer scales, and the bony part of its shell contains large air spaces. This makes the turtle lighter, and helps it float more easily. Soft-shelled turtles also use up less energy when they move, because they do not have to carry a heavy shell around. They move fast, both in water and on land.

FLIPPER FEET

River turtles use their flat, webbed feet to push themselves through the water, in the same way that we use flippers to help us swim. This young big-headed turtle paddles with all four legs. The soft-shelled turtle uses its front flippers to propel itself along, and its back feet mainly for steering.

The large eyes keep a lookout for food and enemies.

This big-headed turtle cannot pull its head inside the shell because it is too large.

The turtle uses its strong, beak-shaped jaws for seizing food, such as snails. Although it has no teeth, it can give a nasty bite.

These thick scales help protect the turtle from enemies, such as water birds.

The shell is made of bone and covered with keratin. Our fingernails are made of keratin, too.

RAZOR MOUTH

PIRANHAS ARE OFTEN thought of as killers, tearing their unfortunate prey apart in seconds with their razor-sharp teeth. In fact, piranhas do not really deserve this fearsome reputation. There are many different kinds of piranhas, but only a few of them, such as these young red-bellied piranhas, are killers. Some kinds are completely vegetarian, eating no meat at all. Even carnivorous (meat-eating) piranhas live on fruit and nuts for most of the year. They only turn to meat when plant food is hard to find. Piranhas live in warm, tropical rivers. Most live in small groups of about twelve fish, although one kind gathers in larger groups, called schools. These schools sometimes contain thousands of fish.

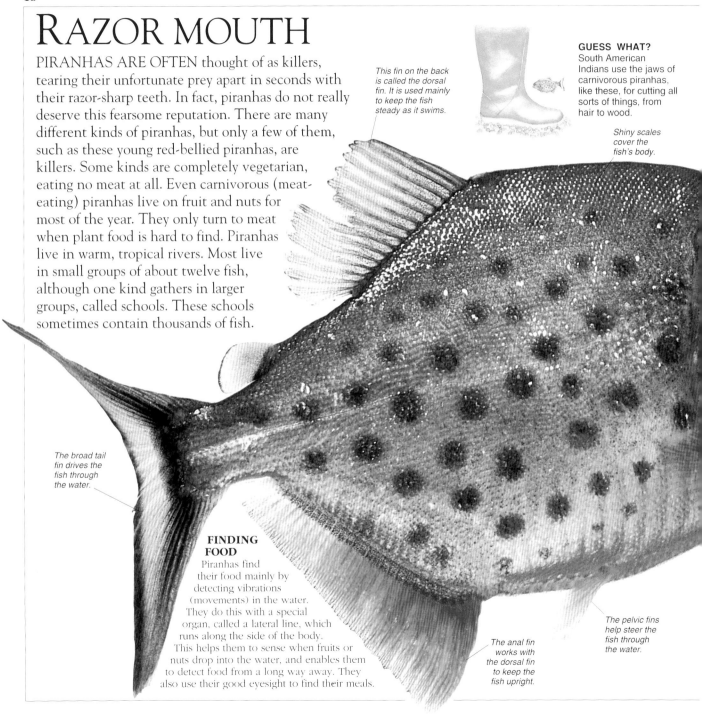

This fin on the back is called the dorsal fin. It is used mainly to keep the fish steady as it swims.

GUESS WHAT?
South American Indians use the jaws of carnivorous piranhas, like these, for cutting all sorts of things, from hair to wood.

Shiny scales cover the fish's body.

The broad tail fin drives the fish through the water.

FINDING FOOD
Piranhas find their food mainly by detecting vibrations (movements) in the water. They do this with a special organ, called a lateral line, which runs along the side of the body. This helps them to sense when fruits or nuts drop into the water, and enables them to detect food from a long way away. They also use their good eyesight to find their meals.

The anal fin works with the dorsal fin to keep the fish upright.

The pelvic fins help steer the fish through the water.

TERRIBLE TEETH

Piranhas have razor-sharp teeth which can easily carve slices of flesh from their victims. The teeth are shaped like triangles, and the top teeth are smaller than the bottom ones. When the fish closes its jaws, the teeth snap together in a strong bite.

The big eyes face forward to detect food and enemies.

MIND YOUR STEP

Carnivorous piranhas such as these sometimes attack other fish. They have even been known to attack animals as large as goats, that have accidentally fallen into the water. They sometimes eat dead animals, too.

The body has flattened sides and is very deep from top to bottom.

The short, broad jaws are very powerful. Strong muscles make them move.

Spotted patterns help disguise the fish.

The huge bottom jaw sticks out farther than the top jaw.

These large nostrils are for smelling food in the water.

This bony cover protects the gills, which take in oxygen from the water.

The pectoral fins help the fish balance, turn, and stop.

BANK MANAGER

THE LONG, BRANCHED roots of alder trees hold the muddy soil of the riverbank together. This prevents the bank from being washed away by swirling currents. The mass of roots also gives the tree a strong grip on the soil, preventing it from blowing over in gusty winds. In spring, before the leaves unfurl, separate clusters of male and female flowers, called catkins, open on the alder tree. If pollen from male flowers lands in the right spot on female flowers, they develop into fruits. These fruits look sort of like pinecones when they are ripe. Seeds eventually fall out of the ripe cones into the river. They are carried along by the water to new stretches of the riverbank, where some will grow into new trees.

These developing catkins contain flowers that will open in the spring.

Ripe fruits are brownish black.

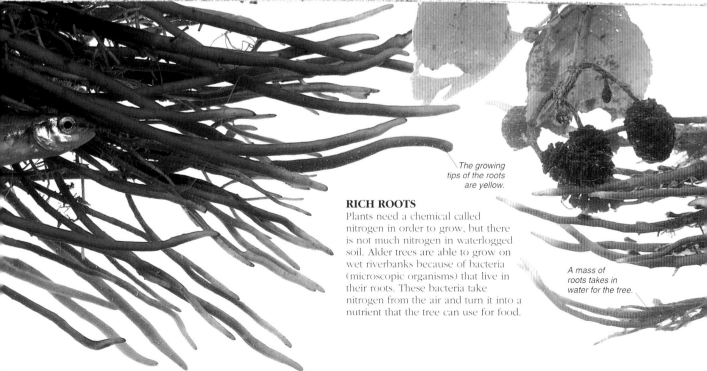

The growing tips of the roots are yellow.

RICH ROOTS

Plants need a chemical called nitrogen in order to grow, but there is not much nitrogen in waterlogged soil. Alder trees are able to grow on wet riverbanks because of bacteria (microscopic organisms) that live in their roots. These bacteria take nitrogen from the air and turn it into a nutrient that the tree can use for food.

A mass of roots takes in water for the tree.

The rounded leaves are broad and blunt with a notch at the tip. They are shiny, and almost hairless.

Each fruit is on a long stalk.

There is at least one seed on each scale.

GUESS WHAT?
Alder wood is often used for wood carving. In the past, people also made gunpowder from the charcoal (burnt wood) of alder trees.

OIL ABOARD
The case around an alder seed contains air, which keeps the seed afloat. There is also a droplet of oil which prevents the seed from filling with water, because water and oil cannot mix. River currents sweep the seed downstream. If it lands in a suitable spot, such as a muddy bank, it may grow into a new tree.

CATKINS TO CONES
Female alder catkins develop into fruits consisting of lots of overlapping scales. These scales contain the seeds. At first the fruits are green, but in autumn they turn brownish black as they ripen. The scales on the ripe fruits open to let the seeds fall out. The empty fruits stay on the bare twigs all through the winter.

These fruits may look like tiny pinecones, but alder trees are not related to pine trees.

Alder trees provide resting places for insects, such as this caddis fly.

Minnows and other fish shelter among the alder roots. Here, they are protected from enemies and from strong currents in the water.

RIVERSIDE TAILS

BROWN RATS ARE VERY adaptable, which means that they can live in all sorts of places. They often make their homes in riverbanks and ditches, where they dig a burrow to live in. The brown rat comes out mainly at night, and often follows the same pathways as it searches for food. It feeds mainly on plants, seeds, and fruit. Brown rats live in a small family group, and each rat has its own place, or rank, in relation to the others. The most important rats have the best food and the best burrows, and they produce more young. Young rats are born hairless and blind, in special nesting burrows. They develop rapidly and, when they are three weeks old, they can scurry around after their mother. By the time they are three months old, they can breed. But most young rats do not survive long enough to breed, because they are killed by enemies such as owls or foxes.

GUESS WHAT?
Thousands of years ago, rats lived only in Central Asia. Then they spread gradually across Europe. Now they live on every continent of the world, except Antarctica. They managed to cross the oceans by climbing aboard ships.

DIRTY RAT?
Rats are often thought of as dirty animals, but in fact they keep themselves very clean. They use their teeth like a comb to straighten out their fur, and they scratch off dead skin and lice with their teeth and claws.

The tail is covered in protective scales.

RATTY PADDLE
Brown rats are excellent swimmers. They use their legs like paddles to push against the water, which makes them move forward. They can dive under water, and swim along below the surface for several yards.

The rounded ears are shaped like funnels, which helps them pick up sounds.

These bright, beady eyes keep a lookout for food and danger.

When the rat is swimming, it holds its tail out of the water. This helps it balance.

The rat uses its feet like paddles to swim through water.

GNAWING GNASHERS
Rats belong to a group of mammals called rodents. All rodents have long, curved front teeth, called incisors, for gnawing. These strong incisors grow non-stop throughout the animal's life. To prevent these teeth from becoming too long, rodents wear them down by gnawing on hard food, such as nuts.

Close up, you can see fur inside the ears. This helps stop dirt and insects from getting in.

SHOCKING SNACKS
Brown rats eat almost anything. Rats that find their way into homes eat household items such as soap, candles, and even plaster. Sometimes rats gnaw through electrical cables, and occasionally give themselves nasty electric shocks.

The long, shaggy fur keeps the rat warm.

The long, sensitive whiskers help the rat feel its way around, especially in the dark.

Brown rats have a good sense of smell. They can recognize other rats by their scent.

The thick, rough outer fur sticks together in clumps when it is wet.

The rat uses these sharp claws to dig burrows, and to grip on to slippery stones and water plants.

SWIMMING SNAKE

THIS VIPERINE WATER SNAKE is well suited to its watery life. It swims easily across the surface of the river, bending its long, streamlined body from side to side, like an eel. These snakes eat a lot of fish, but also feed on frogs, worms, and sometimes newts and toads. They spend a lot of time in the water, but they come out on to dry land to bask in the sunshine, and to hibernate during the winter. Viperine water snakes also mate and lay their eggs on land. The female snake lays up to 35 eggs, under piles of leaves or other plant material. The eggs have leathery shells that prevent the young snakes inside from drying out while they develop. As soon as they hatch, the young water snakes have to fend for themselves.

SCALY SKIN

The outer layer of a snake's skin is made up of thick scales. These are made of the same substance as our fingernails, called keratin. The scales overlap, which helps the snake move easily. From time to time, the snake sheds its outer skin. This is called molting. The skin often peels away in one piece, revealing a shiny new one underneath.

DEADLY DIVER

Viperine water snakes often dive down beneath the surface of the river in search of a meal. They are excellent underwater swimmers, and can hold their breath for long periods of time as they chase after fish and other prey. When the snake catches a meal, it swallows it alive.

The protective scales fit together like a patchwork quilt.

GUESS WHAT?

If the viperine water snake is threatened by a predator, such as a bird, it releases a foul-smelling liquid that oozes out of its rear end. This may put off the attacker, so the snake can escape.

Two nostrils at the tip of the snout help the snake detect its prey. This snake has a good sense of smell.

WHOLESOME MEALS
Like all snakes, water snakes swallow their food whole. To eat a large meal, such as a frog, the water snake has to open its mouth very wide. It can do this because the bones that make up its jaws can each move separately. The snake grips its food with its sharp teeth, which point backward into the mouth. This makes it almost impossible for prey to wriggle away.

These jaws can open very wide to swallow prey whole.

The eyes cannot see well, but the snake's eyesight is good enough to spot moving prey.

There are no eyelids, so the snake cannot shut its eyes.

Snakes have no outer ears, and cannot hear as we do. But they can pick up vibrations through the ground and the water.

This mottled coloring helps the snake blend in with its surroundings.

The snake's flexible body makes it a good swimmer.

WATER WINGS

THE DAUBENTON'S BAT SWOOPS low over the river to snatch a meal of flying insects. It often hovers just above the surface of the water, like a swallow. In summer, these bats usually roost in tree holes in woodlands and parks close to rivers and ponds. Sometimes they make their homes in attics. They leave their roosts at twilight, and head for their watery hunting grounds nearby. There they feed on gnats, moths, and mosquitoes, which they eat in midair. Like us, bats are mammals, and a female bat feeds her young milk produced in her body. Female Daubenton's bats give birth to one young, which stays in the roost's bat nursery with the other young bats. Male Daubenton's bats play no part in rearing the young. After three weeks, the young bat can fly, and follows its mother on hunting trips.

GUESS WHAT?

Most kinds of bats hang upside down from the roof of a cave or tunnel when they hibernate. But Daubenton's bats sometimes hibernate under stones on the floors of caves and old mine tunnels.

BATTY SOUNDS

Daubenton's bats hunt at night, so they need to be able to find their way around in the dark. To do this, they make high-pitched squeaks, and wait for the sounds to bounce back from nearby objects, like an echo. The time that this takes tells the bat the size of the object, and how far away it is. This is called echolocation.

There is a claw at the tip of the thumb for gripping surfaces.

The wings are made of stretchy skin and muscle. They are more flexible than birds' wings.

Long finger bones support the wings.

These ears are like radar dishes. They pick up the high-pitched echoes made by the bat.

The small eyes cannot see very well.

Strong, sharp teeth crush up insects.

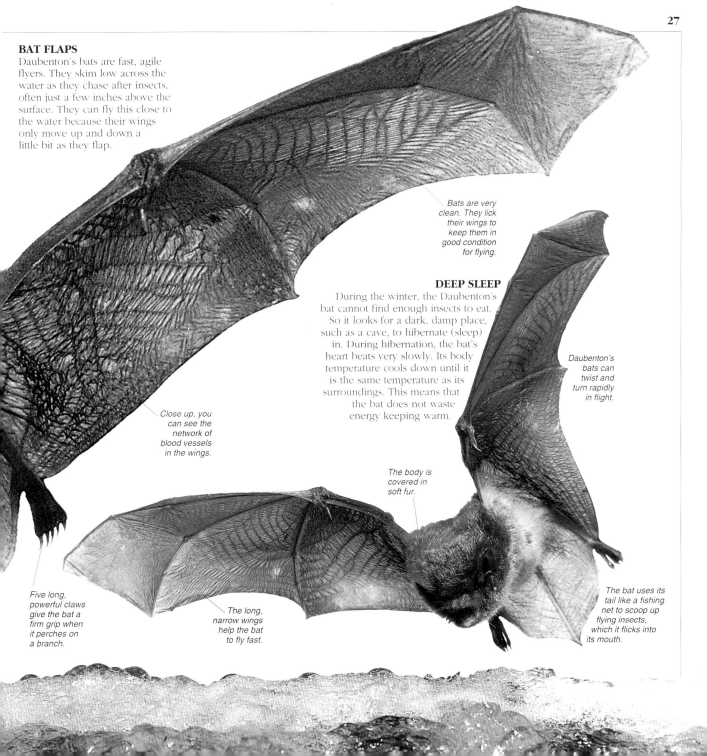

BAT FLAPS

Daubenton's bats are fast, agile flyers. They skim low across the water as they chase after insects, often just a few inches above the surface. They can fly this close to the water because their wings only move up and down a little bit as they flap.

Bats are very clean. They lick their wings to keep them in good condition for flying.

DEEP SLEEP

During the winter, the Daubenton's bat cannot find enough insects to eat. So it looks for a dark, damp place, such as a cave, to hibernate (sleep) in. During hibernation, the bat's heart beats very slowly. Its body temperature cools down until it is the same temperature as its surroundings. This means that the bat does not waste energy keeping warm.

Daubenton's bats can twist and turn rapidly in flight.

Close up, you can see the network of blood vessels in the wings.

The body is covered in soft fur.

Five long, powerful claws give the bat a firm grip when it perches on a branch.

The long, narrow wings help the bat to fly fast.

The bat uses its tail like a fishing net to scoop up flying insects, which it flicks into its mouth.

RIVER DANCER

MAYFLIES ARE FOUND near rivers all through the summer, not just in the month of May, as their name suggests. Mayfly larvae (grubs) live for a year or more under water, but once they have become adults, they only survive for a few days. To attract females, the males fly up and down over the water, dancing around in large groups, called swarms. The females lay their eggs about an hour after mating. They either drop them in the water, or lay them under water on plants or stones. The mayfly larvae that hatch out feed mainly on water plants. They molt (shed their skin) up to 25 times. When the winged mayfly finally emerges, it is still not quite an adult. The wings are dull and smoke-colored, and are covered with fine hairs. After only a few hours (sometimes only minutes), the mayfly molts once more. This time a full-grown adult emerges with shiny, transparent (clear) wings. Mayflies are the only insects that molt after their wings have developed.

LARVA LARDER
An adult mayfly does not eat at all during its short life. It stores food in its body while it is a larva, and this has to last the mayfly through its adult life. The adult's mouthparts are very small, so they are no use for eating. They are used to swallow air, which inflates the stomach. This makes the mayfly lighter for flying.

When the mayfly rests, it holds its wings out above its back. It cannot fold them down over its body.

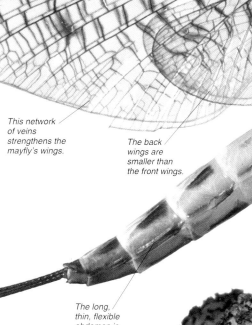

This network of veins strengthens the mayfly's wings.

The back wings are smaller than the front wings.

GUESS WHAT?
Mayflies are sometimes called dayflies, because their lives are so short. There are some kinds of mayflies that live for just a few hours.

TRIPLE TAIL
Mayflies have two or three long tails, called cerci, at the tip of the abdomen (the rear part of the body). The tails help the males balance in the air during their courtship dance. Most mayfly larvae have three tails, too, which help them swim under water.

These three tails (cerci) help the mayfly balance as it flies.

The long, thin, flexible abdomen is divided into segments.

The short hairlike antennae (feelers) sense the mayfly's surroundings.

These large compound eyes are made up of many separate lenses.

There are six jointed legs for holding on to plants.

The thorax is large because it contains the muscles that move the big front wings.

ACID ATTACK

Many kinds of mayfly larvae cannot live in polluted rivers. They die if there is not enough oxygen in the water, or if there is too much acid from acid rain. Acid rain is caused when gases from power stations and vehicle exhausts mix with water in the air. As a result of this pollution, the mayfly has died out in many rivers. Mayflies are an important food for fish, and if the mayflies disappear, the number of fish in a river drops, too.

GLOSSARY

Abdomen *the rear part of the body*
Antennae *a pair of feelers*
Carnivorous *meat-eating*
Compound eyes *eyes consisting of many separate lenses*
Court *to try to attract a mate*
Exoskeleton *a tough covering on the body, made of a substance called chitin*
Gills *the organs that fish use to take in oxygen from the water*
Hibernate *to rest or sleep during the cold months of the year*
Incisors *the chisel-shaped teeth at the front of an animal's mouth*
Keratin *the substance that makes up hair, fur, nails, and hooves*
Larva *the young, grublike stage of an animal's life*

Lateral line *the line of sensitive pits along each side of a fish's body*
Microscopic *too small to see without a microscope*
Molt *to shed the skin or exoskeleton*
Nutrient *a nourishing substance*
Organism *any living animal or plant*
Perch *a resting place*
Pollen *the dusty powder produced by many flowering plants for reproduction*
Pollute *to damage or contaminate with harmful substances*
Roost *to rest or sleep, often in a high place*
Swimmerets *special legs on crustaceans used for swimming*
Thorax *the middle part of the body, containing the heart and lungs*

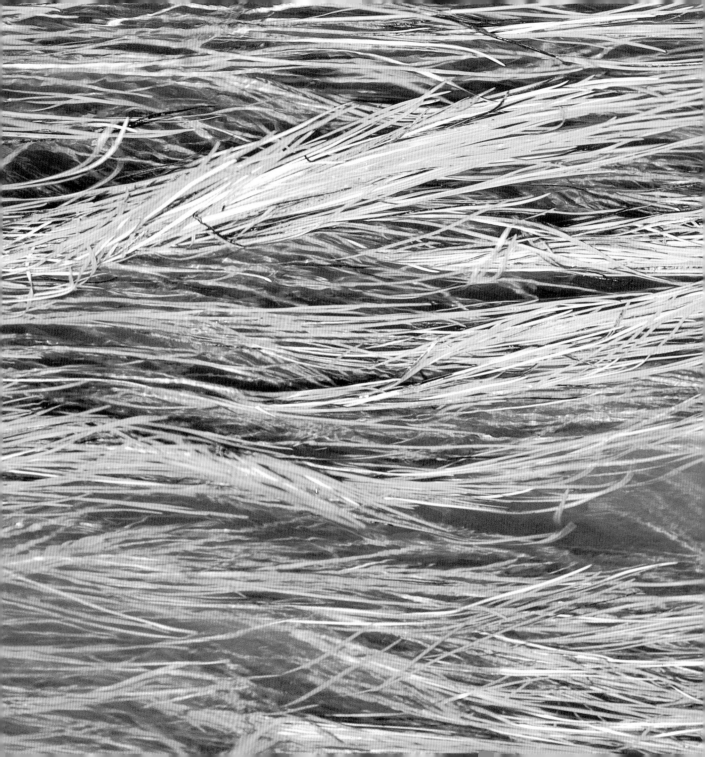

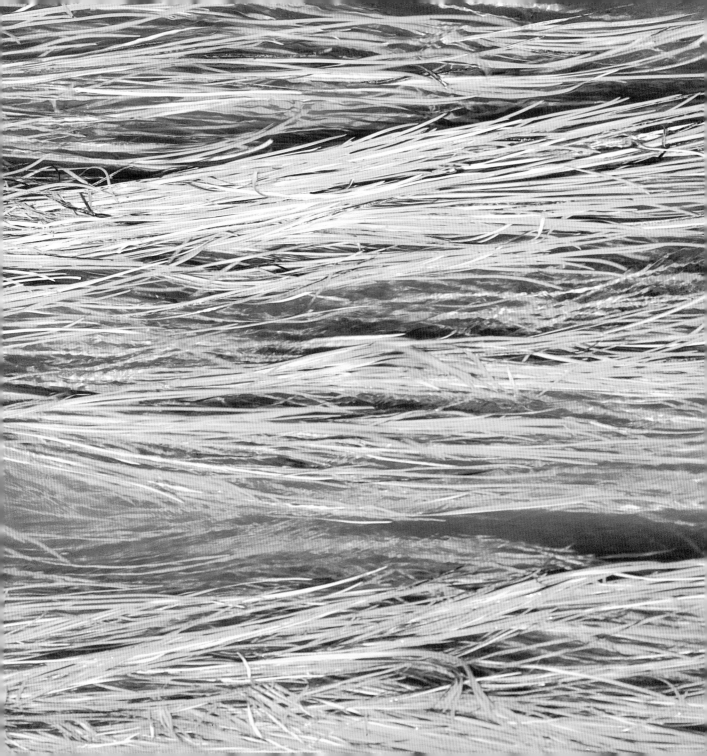